BOBBY LEE

MY DAD MY HERO

GLENDA J. CARTER

Archway Publishing books may be ordered through booksellers or by contacting:

Archway Publishing
1663 Liberty Drive
Bloomington, IN 47403
www.archwaypublishing.com
844-669-3957

Because of the dynamic nature of the Internet, any web addresses or links contained in this book may have changed since publication and may no longer be valid. The views expressed in this work are solely those of the author and do not necessarily reflect the views of the publisher, and the publisher hereby disclaims any responsibility for them.

ISBN: 978-1-6657-3713-5 (sc)
ISBN: 978-1-6657-3711-1 (hc)
ISBN: 978-1-6657-3712-8 (e)

Print information available on the last page.

Archway Publishing rev. date: 04/19/2023

Bobby Lee is an imaginative, curious and courageous little soldier. He takes us along on his special missions that he creates to warm his heart until his Dad returns from his 'job'. Put on your boots and jigsaw uniform and come along with Bobby Lee! I'm excited for the next adventure!

- Anita D. Rowland, an Advocate for Children Reading.

A great and adventurous way for the military littles to relate to their parent's job of being in the military!

- Martene L. Carter, Elementary School Teacher

Put on your camo, pitch your tent and march, fly and sail with Bobby Lee as he discovers amazing places like his Army Dad.

- Robert L. Carter, Jr. CW4 U.S. Army (Ret)

Using imagination, Bobby Lee stays connected to his Dad, a Soldier. Imagination takes Bobby Lee on adventures to places his Dad travels to. Imagination is an essential component of childhood, helping children learn important lifelong skills. Children with parent(s) in the Military should give warm welcome to this book.

- Sonya B. Rowland, PhD; Child Psychologist

My dad is a soldier. He's my hero!

I like to see my dad in his tan-and-brown uniform. It looks like a jigsaw puzzle with boots.

I hurry and put on my jigsaw-puzzle shirt and pants. Next, I put on my boots, cap, and backpack.

Clump! Clump! I make marching sounds throughout the house.

When I march through the house, Dad stops to watch me. He stands at attention and grins. Then he salutes me! I am a soldier like him. I salute him back.

Sometimes, when my dad puts on his uniform, Mom takes pictures so we can look at his picture and remember him when he's gone away. It helps us think of him when we feel sad or happy.

When he's home, we play! We go outside, and I tumble and slide down the big hill in our backyard. Dad says he tumbles down hills, too, when he's at work.

Dad and I eat outside in our favorite place—our tent. It looks like desert sand because it's the color of a sandy beach. Dad and I have fun putting the tent up. We make holes in the ground for the pegs and tie strings to them to hold everything in place.

Up! Up! Up! The tent goes up toward the sky.

Down! Down! Down! My side of the tent falls down to the ground. Dad and I laugh, and then we try again. I only need two more pegs to hold our tent up. When it's up, I sit inside and imagine I'm going to all the places my dad travels.

When Dad's on his job, he lives in a big tent with lots of friends. It even looks like our special place.

While Dad's away, Mom and I read lots of books so I can learn about where he lives when he's not home. We know when it's time for Dad to go on an adventure, so Mom and I make every day a special day with each other.

Dad says, "I have an important job. I help keep you and your mom safe in America. My job is also to keep other moms and children safe."

Sometimes Mom and I look up in the sky. "Can Dad see the same clouds and stars that we see?"

"No, Bobby Lee," she says. "But when we see the clouds and sun, Dad sees the stars and moon. And when we see the stars and moon, Dad sees clouds and lots of sunshine."

"That's funny, Mom; how can that be?"

"When it's daylight here, it's nighttime where Dad is."

I smile and believe my dad always knows when I'm looking in the sky. I can almost see him smiling.

I love adventures! I imagine traveling wherever my dad goes, so I put on my jigsaw-puzzle shirt, pants, and boots just like Dad.

I can't forget my cap and backpack full of yummy snacks and everything I need for an adventure.

"Mom," I shout, "I'm going on an adventure! I will stay safe and come back to you!" I grin. That's what Dad always says. Mom kisses me and gives me a big smile.

I run to the tent. I'm ready to take off in the air! I take a bite of my snack, and soon I'm flying in an airplane like Dad. I fly my airplane past a fluffy cloud. I wave at a cloud that looks like an elephant. Below me, I see green, green grass and water as blue as the sky.

A bird whooshes by me, its wings like gliders in the sky, and then there's another one. Soon, a whole flock of geese make a *V* in the sky. I toss a snack at the birds, and they swoop down to catch it.

I'm flying high—higher and higher still. Up! Up! Up! Up in the sky, the air feels cool. I feel it rush past my face.

Water is beneath me, everywhere I look. Soon, I see the ground, like a sugar cookie rising from the water.

"I see land!" I shout.

I make my plane glide toward the land and pull off my cap. It's hot closer to the ground. "Look at the sand!"

Bump! Bump! Kaplunk!

"I made a great landing!" I say.

I look around at all the sand, and it reminds me of the desert where Dad is. I'm shocked to learn it *is* where Dad lives.

"Whew," I say, "it's hot here." I put my cap back on to keep the sun out of my eyes. I pull out a handkerchief from my backpack and cover my face to protect it from the big dust cloud swirling around me.

I see a camel lapping water under a palm tree. I love adventure! I run toward the camel, but the sand is difficult to run on. When I get to him, the camel sits down. I pull and tug, but he never moves.

"He must be resting," I say.

I climb onto his back, and slowly, the camel gets up. His feet seem to sink into the sand, and the humps on his back are big. *Splish-splash.* I hear water swishing inside them. I grasp the camel's long neck as he starts to trot. From where I sit, I can see palm trees and sand that looks like rippling water.

All kinds of animals—including lizards, snakes, birds, and scorpions—live in the desert.

Sweat runs down my face and neck. "It's too hot out here!" I yell.

How I would love some cool water and a snack.

I trot along on the camel until I see a large boat in the water. I love adventure! I'll just travel on a boat, like Dad.

The wind starts to whip, and suddenly, I'm on an old boat. The sails flap and snap in the wind. I grab the boat's wheel and steer across the ocean's waves.

My dad travels on a boat, and lots of clear blue water splashes against the boat. The rolling waves make the boat jump up and down.

"That tickles!" I say, laughing out loud. My stomach feels full of butterflies.

The wind blows so hard on my face that it almost takes my breath away. Dolphins and whales gracefully dive into the waves. They look at me like they know who I am.

Water, water! It's everywhere. So this is what Dad sees on his adventure. A wave sloshes on me, and I am cooled off from the hot sun.

I turn the boat around so I can see the whales swimming around in a circle. They must be a family. They all look alike and follow each other. They stay close together. The biggest whale must be the dad because he's taking care of the smaller ones. The other whales are big, but not as big as the daddy whale.

The family swims off, and I start to think of Mom. I'm ready to end my adventure.

I run to the back door and shout, "I'm back, Mom!"

She looks at me with a grin and says, "Bobby Lee, you made it back just in time for your special call."

When the phone rings, we both race toward the ringing sound. "Hello, Bobby Lee," the voice says.

"Dad," I say, almost out of breath, "I had another adventure today!"

Dad says, "Great, son! I love an adventure! I am coming home to start a new adventure.

My new adventure will be keeping us safe. There is a virus that's going around the whole world, and all the nations need to help one another be safe. We will all look a little different because we will be wearing masks.

And washing our hands will be very important in keeping us safe from the virus."

"Bobby Lee, let's make up a handwashing song before Dad gets home; that will be fun."

Bobby Lee starts singing his new handwashing song.

"Wetting my hands with trickling water,

using my soap to make bubbles,

I see bubbles all over my hand!

Cleaning my fingers, the back of my hands, and the palms.

Clap! Clap! I see bubbles floating all around.

They burst before I can catch one.

Shake! Shake! Those germs are gone."

Mom says, "Bobby Lee, dad will love this song because we will be doing our part to stay safe". The doorbell rings! It's Dad! My Hero!

ABOUT THE BOOK

Bobby Lee's dad is in the military. When he leaves, Bobby Lee likes to wear boots and tan and brown shirt and pants with his backpack which reminds him of a jigsaw puzzle just like his dad's. He goes to their special place, the brown tent that is filled with lots of books and reads about different adventures. He imagines being in an airplane and seeing geese flying in the air. He see mounds of sand the look like a sugar cookie. He imagines jumping on a camel's back as it laps water under a palm tree. He cannot wait to share the adventures when his dad calls home. Dad talks to Mom and Bobby Lee about a virus and we will need to wear a mask to protect our selves and others.

AUTHOR BiOGRAPHY

Glenda and husband Robert currently reside in McDonough, Ga. Their children loved to hear stories about their dad's military travels and through writing brought them to life. She attented writing courses at Emory University and Kennsaw State University. She published "I am a Soldier's wife" for home life Magazine and was a Paraprofessional at Ware Elementary Fort Riley, Ks.

Printed in the United States
by Baker & Taylor Publisher Services